HOW TO ATTRACT THE RIGHT GUY

Avoid Situationships, Step into Wifey Energy & Get Him to Commit

THALIA OUIMET

ISBN: 9798876374462

Dedications

I dedicate this book to all the incredible single females
out there that have struggled to find love.
May you find guidance and solace here.

Contents

About the Author:

Thalia Ouimet is the founder of We Met Through Thalia, a high-end bespoke matchmaking agency based out of New York City and Miami. She helps successful business men find their perfect match. With nearly 10 years of experience as a VIP matchmaker and dating coach, she has helped men and women recover from heartbreak, become an effective dater, find love, and navigate the inevitable challenges that come with relationships.

Thalia broke into the industry by working for a matchmaking agency but after a few years decided it was time for her to expand her expertise by bringing her talents to NYC to start her own company. With success in Miami, New York City, Chicago, London and Atlanta, she has helped thousands find love.

When she's not coaching her clients or doing matchmaking duties, Thalia devotes her time to her family, friends, fitness and travel. You can find Thalia on social media @thaliaouimet.

ABOUT THE AUTHOR

Disclaimer

By reading this book, you agree to the following. You understand that the information contained in this book is an opinion and should be read for personal enjoyment only. None of the material in this book is to be considered medical, physical, psychological, sexual or legal advice, nor is this book intended to be a diagnosis, prescription, recommendation or cure for any kind of problem. For issues of a medical, physical, psychological, sexual and legal nature, always seek advice from a qualified professional.

You understand that you're wholly responsible for your own behavior and actions and agree to act ethically and abide by all laws. The author or publisher is not to be held responsible for the consequences of any irresponsible actions.

CHAPTER ONE

Your Energy Introduces You First

When you walk into a room your energy introduces you before you ever say a word. Your energy will either be confident, radiant, magnetic, or insecure, anxious, stressed. Which one do you want to be when you walk into a room? What type of energy do you think a high value man will be attracted to? Yep, you guessed it, a woman who is comfortable in her own skin, who exudes vibrant feminine energy, whose goddess light draws everyone in. That's the type of energy that will attract your dream man. You're probably wondering what a "high value man" is. Well, for me that's someone who is loyal, faithful, successful, handsome, takes care of his health, and is family-oriented.

In this book I'm going to break down powerful practices that will help you attract the man of your dreams. Are you ready to level up? Because, girlfriend, if you want that "High Value Man," you are going to have to step up your game. I've been working with high value men for years and I'm going to reveal the secrets of what these men really want and what makes a girl "wifey."

Are you ready to lean in? Are you ready to change your love life forever? If the answer is yes, then you are reading the right book. Now let's get started.

The #1 most important thing when it comes to dating is... (drum roll)... it all starts within. Yep, I know. Probably not what you expected me to say but believe it or not, it starts with YOU. According to physics, the law of attraction, and psychology, we attract mirrors of OURSELVES. Oh, scary. I know. Which means if we are broken inside we will attract broken men. If we subconsciously fear commitment we will attract non-committal men. If we are whole and confident and loving and in great shape and succeeding in life, guess what...we will attract a man who is whole, confident, loving, and in great shape, succeeding in life. I think you get where I'm going with this.

Let's start with what I like to call the "Self-Audit." This technique is something you can do throughout the year. This Self-Audit is a check-in on your mental health, physical health, and how you feel about dating in general.

Ask yourself these 3 questions:

1. How am I feeling about myself? 1-10 (10 being very confident)
2. How do I feel about my body? 1-10 (10 being in the best shape)
3. How do I feel about dating? 1-10 (10 being I'm very optimistic)

If you ranked yourself at least an 8 out of 10 for all 3 categories, then you are ready to start dating!

If you ranked yourself 7 or below for any of the categories I strongly encourage you to work on yourself before getting back into dating because remember, dating is NOT easy. It doesn't take much to make us feel discouraged, and the last thing we want to do is have you come into the dating market at a 7 and drop down to a 4 after just a month of dating. I want you to feel like the feminine goddess that you are so that you can attract the right guy!

I created a routine/method a while ago for myself to make sure I was on my A-game when I was dating. I call it "The Goddess Routine." These simple and easy steps are researched-backed habits to transform your mindset and will get you back on track to the best version of yourself. Now let's get started:

1. Mirror Work: (This one is my personal favorite.) Mirror work involves looking at yourself in the mirror and repeating positive affirmations or engaging in self-talk to improve self-esteem and self-acceptance. It's a technique used to build self-confidence. For example, look in the mirror every morning before you get in the shower and say: "I am so beautiful," "I am resilient," "I am confident in myself," "I am full of abundance," "I am lovable," "I am open to receiving love."

2. Journaling: Keeping a journal can be a therapeutic practice that allows you to reflect on your thoughts, emotions, and experiences. It can aid in self-discovery, self-expression, and tracking personal growth over time. I highly recommend *The 5 Minute Journal* on Amazon.

3. Affirmations: Affirmations are positive statements that you repeat to yourself to boost self-esteem and rewire your current mindset. They can help foster a more positive and confident self-image. For example: "I am beautiful just the way I am," "I love my body," "I am confident."

4. Meditation: Taking the time to meditate every day is so important for your mental clarity. It's all about finding your inner peace in this crazy world of

dating. My life changed when I started meditating every day because it allowed me to get so grounded that nothing could trigger me during my day-to-day. I highly recommend a 1-to-3-minute guided meditation to start off. You'll find many free guided meditations on YouTube or Spotify.

5. Therapy: Seeking therapy can help you HEAL. Think of therapy as a safe space for you to work through past pain (breakups or betrayal, for example), personal issues, gain insights on current behaviors and thought patterns, and improve your mental and emotional well-being. Therapy can be a valuable tool for building self-confidence and addressing any underlying issues that might be blocking your love life from flourishing. Remember, if we are broken inside we will attract broken men. I did therapy for two years to heal my heart and it has paid off.

I know this "Goddess Routine" might seem overwhelming or even daunting, but if you do all 5 of these simple tasks, you will be vibrating on a different frequency. And what I mean by that is, girlfriend, you will have that divine feminine "I'm a boss" Taylor Swift glow, and if you're not a Swiftie that's okay. Just know if you do the work on yourself *cough cough* do the Goddess Routine...you will have that confident, radiant, beautiful, magnetic Goddess glow. In fact, I can assure you even your close friends and family will see your new glow.

I say all of this with so much conviction because when I did the inner work my entire life changed. Not only did I attract better men, I also attracted better people in my life. To put it in the simplest terms, I felt like I was on *The Bachelorette* and I had a line-up of high value men at my doorstep. Are you feeling ready to be the next Bachelorette and have disposable men at your fingertips?? If the answer is YES, then keep reading.

Take Away

When it comes to dating, you will attract what you are. The men that you attract are simply mirrors of yourself. The more work you do on yourself, leveling up your mental health, your physical health, and your mindset, the better your experience will be in dating.

Exercise

What is a "High Value Man"? Well, for me that's someone who is loyal, faithful, successful, handsome, takes care of his health, a family man, and someone with faith. Everyone has their own preferences, so I challenge you to take this time to write down your High Value Man qualities.

CHAPTER TWO

Stepping Into Your Feminine Energy

Now that you have completed the "Goddess Routine" and you are feeling fabulous, it's time to embark on your quest for love. The first practice I want to cover is the power of feminine energy and the role it plays when it comes to dating.

When I say tap into your inner feminine energy, think of Sarah Jessica Parker's Carrie Bradshaw vibe from *Sex and the City*. It's all about a woman who knows her worth and carries herself with a quiet confidence. She's like a flower in full bloom, radiant and captivating. Her energy isn't loud or overbearing; it's more like a subtle perfume that lingers in the air, leaving a trace of grace and elegance wherever she goes. Yes, her heels might be bold and her outfit is chic, but her ENERGY is soft and full of life.

Tapping into your feminine energy is like embracing the softer, more delicate aspects of femininity. Think of it as the gentle yet powerful force that flows through a woman, like a serene stream or a gentle breeze. This energy is all about embracing the unique qualities that make women special and magnetic for men!

For more context about how powerful the feminine energy can be, I figured I'd share a quick story about my dating experience in New York City. This story I'm about to tell you is how I went from masculine energy and not succeeding with men to feminine energy and attracting all the high value men.

I'm in full entrepreneurial mode starting my new company, like a true girl boss in my chicest power suit, taking on the Big Apple with unstoppable energy. This is what I like to call my "Boss Babe Era" – full of ambition, drive, and a go-getter attitude. It was all about making those tough decisions, leading meetings, and onboarding new clientele. Think of it as strutting down 5th Avenue in your favorite heels, matcha latte in hand, conquering the world one step at a time.

But then, there was this lightbulb moment in my own dating life. I realized that the same energy that makes me a powerhouse in the boardroom isn't quite sparking the right kind of chemistry on dates. It was because I had LOST MY FEMININE ENERGY! I was all in my masculine energy!!

That's when I started this journey of self-discovery, kind of like a makeover montage in a rom-com. I realized that maybe, just maybe, it's time to embrace another side of myself and come home to my soft, gentle, feminine side. It's not about losing your boss babe vibe; it's about complementing it with the softer hues of your personality. It's like switching from a bold red lipstick to a soft pink gloss – a subtle but impactful change.

You're probably wondering how the heck I did this. Well, I turned to meditation, which is like your personal fairy godmother helping you transition from work mode to date mode. Each meditation session is like slipping out of your work heels and into your cute, comfy furry slippers. It's about setting the scene for your own transformation, surrounded by candles, soft music, and maybe even a little bit of that dreamy, floral Chanel scent you love.

As I meditated, I wasn't just relaxing; I was reconnecting with my inner goddess. It's like letting your hair down, literally and figuratively, and stepping into this beautiful, soft glow of femininity. Don't get me wrong, you're the same ambitious woman, but now with a sprinkle of romance, ready for love and laughter.

And girlfriend, let me tell you, it worked! On dates, I was no longer just the boss babe from the office; I was this fascinating blend of strength and softness. It's like showing up in a black silk dress that whispers elegance and warmth. My dates were getting a glimpse of my full, dynamic self – the powerhouse entrepreneur by day and the gentle, charming companion by night. I went from not being able to get past a third date to my dates wanting to put a ring on it! Crazy how just shifting into feminine energy can make a huge difference in your love life.

The lesson in this story is about embracing the full spectrum of who you are – a fabulous, multifaceted woman who can rule the boardroom and melt hearts with equal flair. It's a tale of self-love, versatility, and the enchanting dance between different facets of your personality.

Take Away

It's important to come home to your feminine energy once you get done with work. You must set an intention to be in your feminine energy to captivate high value men. I recommend doing a guided meditation every time before going on a date. This will calm your nerves and get you in the right headspace. Men love women who are in their feminine. Your level of feminine energy will dictate the type of men you attract.

Exercise

Take this time to reflect and journal below how you feel after a workday then write down ways that you can shift into your feminine energy. For example: Journaling, doing a guided meditation, playing music or taking a bubble bath.

CHAPTER THREE

Be Bold And Claim What Is Yours

Let's start with the obvious. Most of you reading this probably think that men should make the first move, right? Well, sister, I'm right there with you. I've always believed that the power lies in being chosen. It felt like a game where the men were the seekers and we, the women, were the prizes to be won. That is, until I stumbled upon an intriguing perspective that forever changed my dating life. And when I say forever changed my dating life, what I really mean is if you don't try this new approach YOU ARE MISSING OUT.

One Sunday evening in Manhattan, curled up with a cup of tea, I found myself watching this video online about how back in the day (we're talking like Victorian era) WOMEN CHOSE MEN. Yes, you heard me correctly. WE CHOSE MEN. Let me explain. So imagine this, a woman, elegantly dressed, strolling through a park. She spots a charming gentleman and "accidentally" drops her handkerchief before continuing on her way. The man, believing he's seizing the opportunity, picks it up and rushes after her to return it. Little does he know, he is part of a carefully orchestrated plan. She chose him, not the other way around.

This revelation was a lightbulb moment for me. I had always clung to the idea that being "old-fashioned" meant waiting for a man to make the first move. But here was historical evidence suggesting that women of the past were far from passive; they were strategic and empowered in their pursuit of love. I decided to embrace this "handkerchief" approach in my own dating life and girl, let me tell you. GAME changer! Don't get me wrong, I wasn't being too forward; I was merely using subtle gestures that gave men opportunities to feel like they were in the driver's seat, even when I was the one steering.

This new approach to dating felt empowering. It was a blend of embracing my feminine charm and taking control of my romantic destiny. And the best part? It was fun, like a playful game from the Victorian era, reimagined for the modern woman.

Okay, quick story time to give you some real-life context on how great this trick works!

I was in Notting Hill, at this cozy speakeasy, surrounded by four of my beautiful girl friends. Despite their beauty, they were all a bit frustrated about how guys weren't approaching them. So, I decided to shake things up a bit.

Leaving our table, I went up to the bar, striking up a conversation with the bartender. I confided in him about my little plan – I was going to try and get the phone number of this attractive guy over there on the left. We had a deal: if things went south, I'd wink at him, and he'd come to my rescue.

Positioning myself at the bar, I pretended to look over the drink menu. Casually, I glanced to my left and started up a conversation with one of the guys about his drink choice. This is me dropping a modern day handkerchief. He replied "I got an old fashioned. They do a really good job here," he told me. My response was breezy yet interested. "Oh, I love old fashioneds. I didn't know they had them here."

While we chatted, I was careful with my body language. I stood with one foot facing the bar and the other slightly towards him – a stance that's engaging but not too assertive. We dove into a pleasant conversation about the mixology, where I was from and a few other things.

After about five minutes, I excused myself, mentioning

that I was neglecting my friends and needed to get back. That's when he made his move, saying, "Wait, before you leave, take my number. I'd love to take you out sometime." And just like that, I had successfully dropped the handkerchief, and he had eagerly picked it up.

It was only after he showed his interest by asking for my number that I fully turned to face him, signaling my reciprocal interest. In that moment, I was the orchestrator of the encounter, gracefully guiding the interaction while allowing him to feel in charge of the pursuit. It was a dance of subtlety and confidence, played out in the heart of Notting Hill.

Here's another real-life story.

I was at the Soho Grand in New York City. I was hanging out in the hotel lounge, sipping on my favorite drink, when I spotted this totally dreamy guy across the room. I wanted to get on his radar, but he was with a big group of friends. I decided to use my secret weapon: non-verbal flirting, or as I like to call it, the G.E.S.E. (Grin, Eyes, Seductive Energy)!

So, I flipped my hair, gave him my warmest grin, and did the whole two to three-second seductive stare. This trick like magic, I swear. I read somewhere that 55% of communication is non-verbal, and that it takes up to five times for a man to notice someone is dropping a hint. I had to give him the G.E.S.E. trick like four times, but then – bam! – he noticed.

He finally walked over and was like, "Was it just me, or were you trying to get my attention?" And I, with all my goddess feminine energy, was like, "Well, it depends. Are you single?" And guess what? He was!

We ended up having the most amazing chat, and he even asked me out for dinner later that week. Can you believe it? So, ladies, remember: you can totally drop the handkerchief from across the room, the bar, or even your own table. It's all that grin, eye contact, and a dash of seductive energy. The more you do it, the more fun and confident you'll feel!

Take Away

Back in the Victorian Era women dropped handkerchiefs to make the first move. In modern day dating it's okay to also make the first move. I highly recommend creating an opportunity for a man to his show interest. In the stories above, all I did was open the door and let him walk through it. Believe it or not men are super intimated to walk up to a group of girls. It is up to us to create an environment for a guy to ask us out!

Always drop the handkerchief and make the first move. I promise you won't regret it! Step into your powerful feminine energy and claim what is yours!

For advanced dating advice on attracting the right man, DM me the word "READY" on my Instagram @ thaliaouimet to sign up for my online course!

Exercise

Write down all the places you've noticed good-looking men go to. Think of your ideal type of guy. Is he at a speakeasy? Is he at the gym? Is he on the tennis courts? Is he at a steak house? Is he at a private members club? Is he at a coffee shop? Is he at the park with his dog?

Once you have written this list, I want you to plan on visiting those places and put yourself out there to meet Mr. Right!

CHAPTER FOUR

Let Your Gut Feeling Guide You To Mr. Right

Intuition – you know, that little voice inside your head that sometimes whispers and sometimes screams? Well, I've totally had those moments when it's like every fiber of my being is waving red flags, telling me to just get out of a situation. It's like this superpower we all have for our day-to-day life choices. And oh boy, do I believe in using it, especially when it comes to dating!

You see, our intuition is like our personal cheerleader, always rooting for what's best for us. It's like having a heart-to-heart with your best self. I mean, sure, we all love using our friends for advice, asking for their take on Mr. Maybe-Right. But, let's be real, tapping into our feminine energy is all about that self-confidence and listening to our own gut feeling.

Our bodies are like these amazing truth detectors. They just know when someone is Mr. Wrong, even if he's Mr. Looks-So-Right. If your gut is throwing up warning signs, girl, you better listen. Red flags aren't cute accessories to collect; they are stop signs!

For some context here's a quick story! I'm in my late 20s, living the New York City dream. One day, I met this incredible guy through a friend, and we decided to go on a date. There I am, sipping on a delicious espresso martini, sitting across from this tech guy who seems to tick all the boxes. He's undeniably handsome, successful, the perfect age, kind, family oriented and we are having great banter. The date is going exceptionally well, and I'm having the best time.

But then, something strange happens. After the date, despite everything seeming perfect, I have this gut feeling that something's off. It's weird because he said all the right things, and I couldn't fault the date itself. He even asked me out for a second date, which I agreed to.

On our second date, the feeling intensifies. He's making me laugh, asking intentional questions about me and my family, and we're talking about shared interests in sports and future plans. He's painting this picture of ambition and the life he wants to lead, especially about being a present father one day. He's checking off every single box of what I would consider my ideal guy.

However, my intuition is screaming that this guy is not for me. I have zero evidence, but something feels OFF. After some reflection and meditation post-second date, I just couldn't shake this feeling. It's my intuition telling me to STAY AWAY.

A few days later, the truth came out. I found out that he's been the player of Manhattan, going on different dates every night. I was shocked! My intuition knew all along that this guy wasn't looking for anything serious. It's a classic case of gut feeling versus surface-level perfection. This was a lesson for me to learn to trust instincts especially when it comes to dating.

Despite this let-down with the tech guy, the good news is our gut feeling is always right and it is always with us anytime, anywhere. And did you know you can actually amp up YOUR intuition game? It's like leveling up in being self-aware about those gut feelings. Want to know how to boost your intuition? Well, here's a fun and fabulous way to do just that!

Let me tell you about this game changer for boosting your intuition. I call it tapping into my inner knowing. The easiest way to do that is through meditation. Just 1-3 minutes per day of meditation can seriously up your intuition game. It's all about getting cozy with the convo between your mind, body, and soul.

If you're thinking, "Meditation? Me? No way!" I was totally in the same boat. I only started meditating a few years ago, and let me tell you, it's a total level-up for life. Not only does your intuition get sharper, but there are so many other fab benefits. We're talking stress reduction, better focus, all the good vibes!

Here's a pro tip: start small. Even one minute of meditation can kickstart your journey. Remember learning a new skill is just like anything else. You can't expect to be the next Serena Williams after five tennis lessons. New skills take time and commitment.

Take Away

As you know, there are tons of men out there pretending to be Mr. Right, but they're really not. That's why it's super important to trust your gut and use your intuition. Give a guy time to show his true colors. If you spot red flags or get that funny, off feeling in your gut – listen to it! Your intuition is your number one BFF in the dating world. So, use it and trust it, because it's all about finding someone who's as fabulous as you are!

For advanced training on attracting the right man and learning how to tap into your intuition,

DM me the word "READY" on my Instagram @ thaliaouimet.

Exercise

Ask yourself after a date, how I feel around this person?

Did I see any red flags? If so, what are they.

Does my body feel safe around this person?

Do I feel like this person is trustworthy?

Do I feel heard or did he do all the talking?

Does this person make me feel anxious? If so, why?

Any additional thoughts or feelings you want to journal after a date:

CHAPTER FIVE

The 10 Dating Commandments

Remember those dreamy movie scenes and picture-perfect social media posts? Let's ditch them for a moment. They are fun to watch, but they're about as realistic as a unicorn riding a bicycle. We're dealing with real life here, where every date isn't a candlelit dinner under the stars (though that does sound nice!).

Now, let's talk about our well-meaning parents and friends. Bless their hearts, they try to help, but sometimes their advice feels like it's from another century. We love them, but it's our journey, our rules.

Here's the fun part: dating is not just about finding Mr. Right. It's about discovering yourself, your likes, dislikes, what makes you tick, and what gives you the "ick." It's about those awkward first dates, the unexpected laughs, and yes, even the "why did I even bother" moments. They all add up to the fabulous story of you.

Alright, let's talk about the art of dating in today's world. It's like navigating a maze where the prize is finding your dream partner. It's about time we rewrite the rules of this game, and guess what? I've got just the thing for you: The 10 Commandments of Modern Dating! These aren't just tips; they're golden nuggets of wisdom to help you attract the partner of your dreams. Ready to dive in? Let's go!

The 10 Commandments of Modern Dating

1. **Let's reply or call back in a timely manner** – Showing effort and interest goes a long way. Just like you would want him to call you back within the day, I recommend being timely and getting back to him as soon as you can. Games are overrated and the "I'll make him wait" is not going to get you the results you want.

2. **Let's honor our commitments and not cancel last minute** – Please don't be a flake. Men already have to build the courage to ask a girl out. Unless it's an emergency, follow through with your plans.

3. **Let's have a positive mindset when it comes to dating** – The energy you bring on a date is 50% of the outcome (he's the other 50%). Set the intention on having a fun date and let the law of attraction do the rest of the work.

4. **Let's not drink too much** – Ladies, I know that the pre-date glass of wine may help calm some nerves, but I'm here to encourage you to break that habit and instead have one or two drinks at dinner. You want to stay sharp and clear-headed to see if there is real chemistry versus alcohol chemistry. Also, being drunk and sloppy isn't attractive to anyone.

5. **Let's not enter any date with a sense of entitlement** – Men can feel the entitled energy. The "because I'm hot I deserve XYZ" will not lead to true authentic love, nor will it attract a high value man. If you show gratitude and appreciation for his kind gestures you will stand out.

6. **Let's act like a lady** – Just like you want him to be a total gentleman, step into your feminine energy. Be polite, say please and thank you, and most importantly, most men love a classy lady with good table manners.

7. **Let's not act desperate** – Be confident in what you bring to the table. Each date is not a do-or-die situation. Do your best to be your authentic self and remember that whatever is meant for you will not be withheld from you.

8. **Let's not overshare** – This is a BIG one. Telling your date everything you've ever gone through as if he was your therapist is not a good approach. I suggest sharing personal information in small doses as you continue to get to know your date.

9. **Let's not sleep with a man on a first date** – I encourage you to take the time to actually get to know him. I know there are couples out there that do sleep together on the first date and end up

together. Those people are the exception and we are happy for them. But through my experience in working with men, I hear it time and time again that when a woman waits it shows that she is dating with more intention.

10. **Let's be self-aware** – Be aware of how much you are speaking on the date. Aim for 50/50 so you both feel like you're being heard. Try the "microphone toss." If he asks you a question, answer it and then pass back the microphone with "How about you?"

Take Away

Dating is not just about finding Mr. Right. It's about discovering yourself, your likes, dislikes, what makes you tick, and what gives you the "ick." Follow the 10 Commandments of Modern Dating and continue to show up as your best self! Let your gut feeling guide you to Mr. Right.

Exercise

Think back on the last four dates. Which one of the 10 Commandments do you think you need to work on the most?

Which one of them do you think you do the best at?

Write down the one you want to do better and how you plan to do so.

CHAPTER SIX

First Impressions Count

Here's the secret sauce to leave a lasting impression and totally stand out. First things first, let's talk about your presence. When you're out with Mr. Potential, make it all about the moment. In other words, be present!

Now, let's talk about the cardinal sin of first dates – the cell phone. In a world where we text more than we talk, keep that phone tucked away in your clutch. Let's face it, a picture of your avocado toast or a Boomerang of clinking glasses might be Insta-worthy, but it's not worth missing a moment of real connection.

Next, let's chat about sparkling from the inside out. You know what's truly irresistible? Kindness! Treating everyone, especially our superhero waitstaff, with a sprinkle of kindness and a dash of respect is like wearing an invisible crown. It shows you are not just a pretty face but you have a heart of gold too.

Remember, it's not just about finding a high value man, but being a high value woman. You are a total catch, and your warmth, attention, and grace are your superpowers. Use them well, and watch the magic happen!

Last but not least, the most cringe controversial topic on dating! ... (drum roll)... Are you supposed to offer to split the bill on the FIRST date?? The answer is YES! Ladies, you heard it here first. After years of data from working with men, I am here to tell you that it is always a kind gesture to offer to split on the first date. It gives men an opportunity to step into their masculine energy and demonstrate traditional chivalry by declining the offer and paying the bill himself.

When he graciously takes care of the bill, flash him your warmest smile and say, "Thank you so much for dinner!" Let your gratitude sparkle in your eyes – it's all about making that moment feel warm and genuine. And here's a little pro tip to sprinkle some extra brownie points. When you get home from your date, send him a cute thank you text. Maybe something like,

"Hey Ryan, Thank you so much for dinner. I had a great time."

I promise if you follow these guidelines, you will leave a lasting impression and get that high value man!

Take Away

On a date let's put our best foot forward by being present, staying off our phone, being kind to waitstaff and showing gratitude when he picks up the check. Offering to split the bill on the first date says a lot about you, and him taking you up on it says a lot about him. Ladies, chivalry is NOT dead and a total gentleman will decline your offer and treat you to dinner. Showing appreciation and thanking him once he paid, as well as sending a thank you text after the date, is the best approach to getting a high value man.

Exercise

Below, draft 3-4 thank you texts to have ready for when you get home.

CHAPTER SEVEN

Avoiding Situationships

I was coaching one of my female clients who told me she had been seeing this really handsome, successful guy for months. I proceeded to ask her if he had agreed to commitment. With disappointment, she said no. Let me add here that the guy she was investing her time in had already told her he was not seeking anything serious. For some reason she took that as a challenge and decided to try and win him over. Side note, that is the worst thing you can possibly do. When a man tells you he isn't looking for something serious or isn't looking for a relationship, that is your cue to walk away. Immediately!

She proceeded to try and get him to commit by amping up her game. She started cooking for him, letting him sleep over, taking care of his dog, and basically doing all the girlfriend duties while not having the girlfriend title. This is what I like to call a classic case of a "situationship."

The best way to avoid a situationship from the early onset is to get clarity on what your crush is looking for. It's so important to have this conversation on date one or two or at the absolute latest date three. The reason for this is you don't want to catch feelings for someone who isn't looking for a relationship when you are looking for a relationship. If you are both on the same page about wanting the same end goal, then invest your time in getting to know him. On the off chance that your crush is lying about his agenda and he claims to be looking for a relationship but his actions start to speak differently, that's when you have to walk away. No matter how much you like him, no matter how great the chemistry is, you have to honor your needs.

I created a short list to help you see what are considered girlfriend duties. Avoid doing these things if he is not your boyfriend.

What NOT to do:

- Avoid cooking/baking for men who aren't your boyfriend
- Avoid sleeping over until there is a conversation about monogamy
- Avoid running errands for him or making appointments for him
- Avoid watching his pet while he's out of town
- Avoid booty calls if he didn't plan a date

The biggest thing to remember when it comes to avoiding a situationship is when a guy tells you he isn't ready, listen to him the first time. If he wants to go with the flow or he isn't looking for anything serious, or he isn't over his ex, believe him and WALK AWAY!

Ladies, the best way to encourage him to commit is to take the time to get to know him. Also have him crave those sleepovers and homecooked meals. By leaving the girlfriend duties out of the equation, it will create the energy of him wanting you more.

Take Away

Girlfriend duties are great when you have the girlfriend title. Do NOT give a man the girlfriend treatment before getting commitment. When someone tells you their intentions, believe them the first time. Don't ever invest in someone who says let's go with the flow and just see where this goes. Ladies, anything along the lines of "let's go with the flow" is a red flag. Situationships can almost be avoided 90% of the time if you get clear about intentions. Knowing someone's agenda will help you get better results with dating.

Exercise

Make a list of all the times you've done girlfriend duties without the girlfriend title, and then write a letter to yourself forgiving yourself for those things – forgiving yourself for pouring into someone without getting the result you wanted.

CHAPTER EIGHT

Final Thoughts From Your Favorite Matchmaker

Dating is like embarking on the most thrilling, unpredictable adventure of your life. Imagine this: you're the star in your very own romantic comedy, complete with quirky moments and butterflies in your stomach. But here's the twist – there's no script, no director, and certainly no retakes! It's all about you making the choices that feel right.

Below I created a "How To Attract The Right Guy" recap list of this book to help you navigate dating in the best way possible. Let's begin!

1. **Know Thyself** - Before you even think about dating, get to know who you are and what you want. Your likes, dislikes, deal-breakers, and preferences.

2. **Confidence Is Key** - Walk into that date with your head held high. Confidence is magnetic and attractive!

3. **Honesty Is the Best Policy** - Be your authentic self. Pretending to be someone you're not is a recipe for disaster.

4. **Communication Is Key** - Learn to express your feelings and desires clearly. No one is a mind reader, after all.

5. **Listen To Your Intuition** - Pay attention to what your date is saying and listen to how your gut feels.

6. **Respect Yourself** - If he says he isn't looking for a relationship respect yourself enough to walk away no matter how much you like him.

7. **Don't Rush -** Love can't be hurried. Take your time to get to know your crush and find out his true intention.

8. **Ditch the Drunk Dates -** 1-2 drinks max! You want a clear mind to make a good judgment on your crush. Drinking might allow some red flags to slip.

9. **Be a High Value Woman** - Be punctual, be kind to waitstaff, be present and show gratitude.

10. **Enjoy the Journey -** Dating should be fun, not a chore. Enjoy the process of meeting new people and experiencing new things.

Remember, dating doesn't have to be a daunting task filled with anxiety and confusion. With everything we covered in this book you'll be well on your way to dating with purpose, confidence, and a whole lot of fun. So put on your favorite outfit, flash those pearly whites, and get ready to attract that high value man!

Lastly, I want to leave you with this. I am here to tell you, as a matchmaker, as a dating coach, there is no reason for you to not get the results you want if you just lean in, work on yourself, and follow the 10 dating commandments. You have all the potential in the world to get your dream guy. You are worthy of getting that high value man!

I created this book to give you guidelines and male insights to help you navigate modern-day dating. It doesn't matter which city you live in, whether you're in LA or New York, London or Chicago, Montreal or Atlanta, there are dating challenges in every city. I am here to tell you that if you have a positive mindset towards dating and you cancel all those limiting beliefs about men like, "all the good guys are taken in my city" or "all men are cheaters," then you will succeed. Remember, positivity attracts positive outcomes. There is absolutely no reason for you not to get your dream guy if you follow everything in this book and truly believe that you deserve love. You've got this, girl. I'm rooting for you. xoxo – T

Take Away

Do you want to take your dating game to the next level? If you answered YES for advanced dating advice on attracting the right guy, DM me the word "READY" on my Instagram @thaliaouimet to sign up for my online course!

Exercise

Take this time to reflect and write down the answers to the following questions.

1.) What are 5 things I learned from this book?

Final Thoughts From Your Favorite Matchmaker

2.) What chapter resonated with me the most? Why?

Final Thoughts From Your Favorite Matchmaker

3.) What advice in this book do I plan on sharing with my friends?

4.) What is the #1 thing I learned that surprised me the most.

I hope flipping through these pages felt as enchanting for you as dancing across the keyboard was for me. In this big, beautiful journey of love and self discovery, I send you nothing but wishes filled with wisdom and guiding light. And hey, when you do find your dream guy, don't forget to slide into my DMs on Instagram with the deets—I can't wait to hear all about it! For those craving a little extra guidance on navigating the complex world of dating, my website www.thaliaouimet.com welcomes you with open arms! Now, with a heart full of hope and a spirit of adventure, get out there and call in the love of your life. Xox – T

Made in the USA
Las Vegas, NV
21 February 2024

86052330R00046